The Adventures of a Self-Managing Team

The Adventures of a Self-Managing Team

Mark Kelly

San Diego • Toronto • Amsterdam • Sydney

Library of Congress Cataloging-in-Publication Data
Kelly, Mark, 1955-
    The adventures of a self-managing team / Mark Kelly.
        p.   cm.
    Includes bibliographical references.
    ISBN 0-88390-058-0 (alk. paper)
    1. Work groups.   I. Title.
HD66.K45   1991
658.4'036—dc20   91-71465
                                                          CIP

Pfeiffer & Company
8517 Production Avenue
San Diego, California 92121
Telephone (619) 578-5900
FAX (619) 578-2042

Cover Design: Susan Odelson
Interior Design/Page Composition: Judy Whalen
Artwork: George Hager

This book is printed on acid-free, recycled stock that
meets or exceeds the minimum GPO and EPA
specifications for recycled paper.

*This book is dedicated to
the associates of the
James River Corporation
Kendallville plant.*

ACKNOWLEDGMENTS

Thanks to Dan Napralla and all of the associates of the James River Kendallville Plant for allowing me to be a part of your family over the last three years.

Thanks to Starr Eckholdt and the other consultants of the OSD Alliance who helped to design this organization and facilitate its development. Thanks also to John Miner for his internal consulting support.

Thanks to Jennifer Hinton for your wise editing and to Cynthia Garver, Calico Publishing Associates, for your able assistance in bookmaking.

CONTENTS

PREFACE xi

PART I: FORMING
    1. Application in Process 3
    2. The Job Interview 7
    3. Orientation 11
    4. Technical Training 19
    5. Becoming a Team Member 25

PART II: STORMING
    6. A Leadership Struggle 37
    7. An Unfocused Team Representative
       Council 41
    8. Attendance Problems 47

PART III: NORMING
    9. Making Smooth Shift Transitions 57
    10. Addressing Quality Issues 61
    11. Accelerating Press Changeover 67

PART IV: PERFORMING
    12. Cross-Training in Action 75
    13. The "Event" — Organizational Meshing . . . 79
    14. Creating a Resource Team 83

PART V: TRANSFORMING
    15. Plant Expansion and Team Reformation . . . 91

EPILOGUE 95

APPENDICES

Characteristics of Self-Managing Teams 103
Potential Areas of Responsibility 105
Organization Design Issues 107
Implementation Steps 109
Implementation Suggestions 111
Stages of Team Development 113
References and Additional Reading 116

None of us is as smart as all of us.

Anonymous

PREFACE

Self-managing teams are the most promising and exciting revolution in American companies today. They may be called self-directed teams, high-performing teams, or employee involvement teams. But whatever they are called, they are proving to be the most productive innovation in American industry in years and the wave of the future.

A self-managing team is a group of workers which has a high degree of decision making and problem solving responsibility and essentially manages itself. It is based on the idea that the people doing the work are the experts in those jobs and the best way to manage is to empower them to take charge of their own destiny.

The role of management is turned upside down in this new environment. The manager's job is to lead, empower people, and remove roadblocks that get in the way of the team being able to do its job. The new primary responsibility of the manager is to act as a coach and help teams mature in their development toward self-management.

Many of our most progressive companies are now using or experimenting with self-managing teams, including Proctor & Gamble, GE, Digital Equipment, AT&T, Boeing, Xerox, Westinghouse, Motorola, Ford, James River, Corning, and a variety of small-to-medium sized firms. The number of both manufacturing and service companies moving in this direction is growing dramatically each year.

This is the story of a self-managing team as it lives through the first two years of a new plant start-up. The story is seen through the eyes of the team members as they confront and deal with a variety of issues. The story traces the development of the team as well as the development of the plant during this period.

It is essentially a true story based on actual events of a new plant which began operation in 1987. I have taken some liberties with the characters and the flow of events, but I have been faithful to the spirit of the plant and the types of issues they have faced in their first two years.

Although the story occurs in a new plant, the issues are the same ones that any self-managing team must address whether it is in a new organization or an existing one that is converting to a self-managing team environment. The lyrics may be different, but the music will be the same.

If the concept of self-managing teams is new for you, you may want to read the appendices first to get some more background on what these teams are all about. If you are a member of a self-managing team or you are involved with designing and managing this kind of organization, then read on to experience how one team dealt with the challenges it faced.

Mark Kelly
October 1990

▲ Part I
▼ Forming

Chapter 1

▲▼▲▼

APPLICATION IN PROCESS

Billy Mann came screeching into the driveway in his pickup truck, almost knocking over the trash cans by the curb. He slammed the door of his truck, stomped into the house, grabbed a beer, and went out on the back porch.

His wife followed him. "What's wrong?" she asked.

"Another layoff at the plant," he said looking away from her. "Three weeks this time, maybe six, with inventory so high. It all depends on car sales next month."

Elbows on his knees, he stared at the flaking gray paint on the floor between his feet. "I can't take this any more. This is the third time in two years."

His wife put a warm hand on his neck, massaging it lightly. "What are you gonna do?" she asked.

"I don't know," Billy answered, lifting his beer to take a long draw. "The union can't help. I guess I'll have to look for work."

Billy hated the thought of losing his seniority at the auto parts plant, but he disliked the frequent layoffs more. With kids to feed and bills to pay he would rather have work he could rely on.

So the next day he made an appointment with Mrs. Morris at the unemployment agency. After reviewing his application, the counselor mentioned a new plant in town.

"This isn't exactly your field, but I think it has possibilities," she told him. "Clear Lake has only been in the area six months. They make cereal boxes."

"That doesn't have anything to do with what I've been doing for the last five years," Billy said.

"Well, your technical experience will certainly carry over, but Clear Lake is more interested in the type of people they hire than in previous experience. Another thing that's unique about their system is that there are no supervisors."

"Who runs the factory?"

"The employees. They have what they call self-managing teams."

"That sounds crazy," Billy said, shifting uneasily. "What else have you got?"

"That's it," she said, closing the file. "Nobody is hiring now. And you're not the first person who's been in here asking."

"Okay," said Billy, standing up. "I guess I'm interested. I'll go on and fill out this application so we can set up an interview."

"I have to warn you that applying for this job isn't quite that easy. The plant is hiring twenty-five people and you're one of three hundred applicants."

Billy felt a sinking sensation.

"They plan to cut that number to one hundred before they start interviewing," she continued. "You'll have to take tests for mechanical aptitude, perceptual speed, math skills, and communication skills. If you make it into the final pool, you'll be invited to interview with a team of managers and employees at the plant."

"Sounds like a full-time job just to get in the door," Billy said gruffly.

"Maybe so, but I've heard good things about this place," she said.

Billy took the application with him and set up an appointment to take the tests the very next day.

Later that week, Mrs. Morris called to tell Billy he'd made the first cut. Hunching his shoulder to hold the phone to his ear, Billy jotted down the interview information. When he hung up the phone he let out a war whoop. He already felt a sense of accomplishment just getting past stage one of the screening process.

The next day, Billy and his friend Tim sat talking in Hamburger Palace. "I can't get over how glad I am just to have a shot at it," Billy said. "Listen, you know someone who works there, don't you? Give me the scoop. This place sounds a little weird."

"You're right about that," Tim said. "No supervisors. Everybody wears a uniform, even management. Men and women work side by side and they're always having meetings to hash things out. See over there?" Tim nodded toward a corner table. "I think those are the managers of the plant."

Billy looked at them curiously—three men and a woman dressed in what looked like gas-station uniforms talking intently over cheeseburgers.

Billy frowned. The more he saw and heard about this place, the more uncertain he felt about what to expect.

Chapter 2

▲▼▲▼

THE JOB INTERVIEW

B illy showed up at the plant thirty minutes early to get a look around. As he walked up the stairs, he saw a large poster on the wall.

> ### CLEAR LAKE MISSION STATEMENT
> We are dedicated to providing consistently superior products and services to all of our customers.

The poster had forty signatures scrawled below the message, followed by the words "We Are Clear Lake." As Billy reached the reception desk, he noticed another poster.

> ### OUR PHILOSOHY
> We believe in fostering an environment that encourages superior products and performance, which result from:
> - ☐ Clearly perceived goals
> - ☐ Ongoing communication
> - ☐ Proper application of skills
> - ☐ High standards of decorum and conduct
> - ☐ A clean and safe working environment
> - ☐ Wise use of resources
> - ☐ Shared information

The receptionist told Billy he could get a drink and wait in the lunch area since he was early. As he headed down the stairs, Billy turned sideways to avoid jostling a man whose arms were piled high with rolls of toilet paper.

"Excuse me," said the man. "You must be here for an interview. My name is Dan. Welcome to Clear Lake. I'd like to stay and talk, but I've got to get the bathroom cleaned before we start."

"Start what?" Billy asked.

"The interviews," said Dan. "I'll see you in a while."

Billy thought he remembered seeing Dan at Hamburger Palace the other day. "This place is getting stranger by the minute," he thought to himself.

Ten minutes later Billy was called into the small conference room.

Four people sitting around a table stood to greet him. One of them was Dan, who introduced himself as plant manager.

"Hello again," said Dan. "Have a seat and I'll introduce the rest of the interview team."

Sam and Amy were workers from the plant, or associates as they called themselves, and Spence was from Clear Lake's corporate offices.

"I can see that you're wondering why I was cleaning the bathroom," Dan said. "Everyone who works here is responsible for housekeeping. It was my turn. Now let's talk about you."

For the next hour and a half, the interview team questioned Billy at length. They covered his work history, technical and social skills, strengths and weaknesses, and ability to work as a team member, as well as his reasons for applying to Clear Lake.

Billy was surprised when neither Dan nor Spence led the interview. All the interviewers seemed to be on equal footing.

After all the questions were answered, Dan said, "Billy, you're obviously a talented and dedicated worker. I think you look good as a candidate for our plant." He looked at the other interviewers who nodded in agreement.

"My major concern is whether you'll return to the auto parts plant when they call you back from layoff. We invest heavily in training new people. We can't afford to have you leave after a few weeks on the job."

Billy looked earnestly at Dan. "If you decide to hire me, and if I decide to work here," he said, "I'd resign from the auto parts plant. Right now I want stability and the auto plant isn't delivering it."

"That's what we needed to hear," said Dan.

"However," said Billy, getting up his nerve, "I have some questions for you."

"Fire away," said Dan.

"First, how does the pay system work?" asked Billy.

Amy responded, "You'll begin at the starting salary and then your salary will rise to the level of everyone else over the next six months. You also will be paid for your overtime."

"You mean everybody makes the same thing?" Billy asked.

"There is one level of pay for management and another for all other plant employees," Dan said.

"In addition, we all participate in the plant gainsharing plan which is based on how well we beat our goals in production, quality, safety, and organizational effectiveness," Amy explained.

"If there are no supervisors in this place, who enforces the policies and regulations?" asked Billy.

"We do," Sam said. "Every one of us. We don't really have any written policies yet, but each person on the team is responsible for his own behavior and if someone on a team is not meeting his or her obligations, the members of that team address the issue."

"Well," said Billy, "I'm not used to working in a place where managers trust me to do the job I'm hired to do."

"There is a high degree of trust and respect between management and associates, and among the team members, too," said Amy. "And you couldn't get away with goofing off for long, because we all depend on each other and we're constantly monitoring our progress."

Dan concluded the interview, saying, "Thanks for coming in and talking with us this morning. We'll let you know by the end of the week what we decide."

Billy left the plant feeling that he'd made a good impression. He realized with surprise that he would be disappointed if he didn't get an offer.

Chapter 3

ORIENTATION

Billy waited anxiously for the next three days. When the receptionist called to tell him he had the job he let out a sigh of relief. She told him to report to the plant Monday morning for the first day of his eight-week orientation.

Billy spent the weekend trying to figure out how orientation could possibly last that long.

Monday morning Billy arrived early. When he walked into the conference room he saw about twenty people clustered in small groups. He stood awkwardly to the side, wishing the orientation would begin.

A woman also standing alone smiled at him from across the room. She walked over to him and said, "Welcome to boot camp."

"Boot camp," said Billy. "Do you work here?"

"I do now. I'm Susan, a new recruit," she said, thrusting out her hand.

Billy shook her hand and introduced himself.

"I said 'boot camp' because that's what I thought of when they told me orientation would last eight weeks."

Billy laughed. "I know what you mean. I spent all weekend trying to figure out what we would be doing."

"Well, it looks like the wait is over," said Susan. "Here they come. Fasten your seat belt."

Everyone took a seat. Susan sat down beside Billy and said, "I'm a little nervous. Is it okay if I adopt you as my buddy for orientation?"

"Well, sure," Billy said, "but let me get something straight. I'm married."

"I'm divorced," Susan said straightforwardly. "Don't worry. I'm just looking for a friend."

"Okay, friend," said Billy. "I have a feeling I'm going to need all the help I can get."

Billy looked up and saw Dan, the plant manager, come in with ten people. Billy thought he recognized some of them from that day at Hamburger Palace.

"Good morning," said Dan. "I think you all know me— I'm Dan. These people to the right here, William, Craig, and Annette, are the rest of the Jugglers, the management team. We call ourselves that because it seems like we're always trying to juggle a lot of balls in the air at one time.

"Over here," he said, gesturing to the left, "are Ken, Sue, Kimberly, James, and Louis, the Assimilation Team. They are responsible for showing you how we do things around here and helping you learn the skills to get assimilated into our system. You're going to think a lot about teamwork over the next few weeks. That is the basis for what we do here.

"But before we get started, we have a little ritual to perform, so bear with us while we pass out these keys."

Susan leaned over and whispered to Billy, "These must be the keys to our foot lockers where we keep our uniforms and weapons."

"I don't know," said Billy. "Based on everything else I've seen about this place so far, these might be keys to the executive washroom."

When the keys were distributed, Dan raised a spare key above his head with a flourish. "This is your key to the plant. Clear Lake is your plant now. Welcome aboard."

There was a moment of stunned silence as everyone digested what he'd said. Billy squeezed his key in his hand and felt a surge of excitement.

"We do this to illustrate that we mean what we say," Dan said. "For most of you this will be unlike any job you've ever had. You may have worked in other places that encouraged you to think of co-workers as family. But if it were a family, you were one of the kids and you probably didn't have much say about what went on. Or maybe you were a supervisor who had to keep the others in line. Here at Clear Lake we depend on input from each associate at every stage of the game. Everybody's important and everybody's responsible. But the Assimilation Team will explain all that. I'll leave now and let them do their magic," he said.

The Assimilation Team began by explaining the pay and benefits systems. Plant operations and layout were next on the agenda.

"All teams here operate on rotating shifts. The two printing presses run continuously, always attended by one team," Louis explained. "In addition there's a gluer, a machine that only runs during the day. We have a press support team to handle shipping and support functions. There's also a customer service team that deals with customers, scheduling, and accounting. All teams report to the Jugglers.

CLEAR LAKE ORGANIZATION

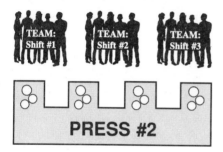

(All teams report to the Jugglers.)

"In addition, everybody takes part in a variety of task force committees, which address issues such as quality, safety, and maintenance. Your team will be responsible for electing its representatives."

After lunch the group toured the plant. Billy noticed Susan looking anxious as she eyed a woman confidently driving a forklift to pick up a pallet stacked high with flattened cartons. Billy couldn't make himself heard over the noise of the press so he just smiled and gave her a thumbs up sign. A few feet away a man adjusted dials on a tall tower of ink. Two women performed a statistical quality test on a product sample at a light table. Billy felt another wave of excitement at the prospect of learning a new job.

But the six-week technical training program wouldn't actually begin for two more weeks, he was told. First came two weeks of training in social skills.

For the next two weeks Billy, Susan, and the other new associates were led through a variety of lectures, exercises, games, demonstrations, and discussions dealing with the development of teamwork and social skills. Topics ranged from consensus decision making and effective communication to conflict resolution and creativity.

On the next to the last day, Kimberly announced that the trainees would be divided into teams of five. Each team would have the afternoon to prepare a skit illustrating important points they had learned.

Susan and Billy ended up in the same group. While Billy and the other three were casting about for ideas Susan was quiet. Suddenly she said, "I've got it! Let's do a skit about the Wizard of Oz. Each of us will be searching for one of the concepts we discussed this week." Everyone agreed and for the rest of the afternoon they worked on the skit.

▲▼▲▼

The next morning all of the teams sat around the side of the room and waited their turn. Billy and Susan's team ended up going last.

Susan stood up and began. "Hello, my name is Dorothy and I'm off to see the Wizard of Oz to find a job that's 'PLORK' ('Play & Work' combined). I'm hoping he can give me the magic answer."

She then looked up and started singing:

"Somewhere over the rainbow
Is a job that's fun.
There's a plant that I read of
In the Chicago Sun,

"Where all the people really care,
Where you keep learning while you're there.
Commitment's high and conflict's rare.
Oh, why can't I work there?"

She pretended to stroll down a road where she met Scarecrow. "Hi," said Dorothy, "I'm going to see the Wizard to find a job that's 'PLORK.' Do you want to come with me?"

"You bet," said the Scarecrow. "I'm looking for a brain. I need a job that will challenge me to think."

They locked arms and walked a little farther where they met Tin Man. "Hi," said Dorothy. "We're going to see the Wizard to find a job that's 'PLORK' and challenging. Do you want to come with us?"

"I sure do," said the Tin Man. "I don't have a heart and I'm looking for a job where I can trust and care about the people I work with."

The three locked arms and walked a little farther where they met the Lion. "Hi," said Dorothy. "We're going to see the Wizard to find a job that's 'PLORK' and challenging and where you care about people. You want to join us?"

"I don't know," said the Lion. "I don't have any courage. I need a job where I can make a commitment, but I'm not sure I can commit to going with you."

"Sure you can," said Dorothy. So they grabbed the Lion and headed off to see the Wizard.

When they got to Oz, they faced the Wizard, played by Billy.

Dorothy spoke up. "We've come to find a job that's 'PLORK' and challenging, where people care about each other and are committed to doing the best they can do. Can you help us find it?"

Billy replied in a booming voice, "I think you have already found it. Just think about your journey here. You did some play and work. You challenged yourselves. You trusted each other and committed yourselves to working together on this project. You demonstrated all of the qualities you are looking for. Now turn and face the audience. Tap your heels together three times and repeat after me:

"There's no place like Clear Lake.
There's no place like Clear Lake.
There's no place like Clear Lake."

As the chanting faded, the audience broke into applause.

Sue, from the Assimilation Team, moved to the front of the room. "Great job everyone," she said. "You all illustrated what we've worked on beautifully. Now, let's head out back for a game of volleyball to finish off the week."

On the way out, Billy stopped Susan. "The guys at my old job would never believe that I was the Wizard of Oz on company time, but I think I got more out of that than anything we've done so far," he said. "I'm starting to see what they mean about working together."

"It was fun," Susan said. "I'm good at this stuff, though. What's got me worried is technical training."

"Don't worry about it," Billy said. "You've been helping me these past two weeks. It's my turn to help you."

Chapter 4

▲▼▲▼

TECHNICAL TRAINING

Next Monday the group gathered again in the large conference room. Ken, from the Assimilation Team, began the session. "For the next six weeks, we'll be involved with technical skills training. Here's a list of the topics we'll be covering," he said, passing out a handout.

Glancing over the sheet, Billy saw that they'd be learning about all phases of the plant like press operation, quality control, safety, forklift driving, problem solving, administrative procedures, and customer service. At the bottom of the list he saw the phrase "The Bible." He was puzzled, so he raised his hand and asked, "What is this 'Bible'?"

"You're one step ahead of me," Ken said. "But now is as good a time as any to pass them out." When everyone had one of the three-inch binders, Ken resumed his explanation.

"This is what we call 'The Bible.' It's the documentation of all our technical processes and includes the standard operating procedures, potential problems, trouble-shooting checklists, and a basic explanation of all of the equipment. It will be your best friend over the next six weeks."

WORK PROCESS

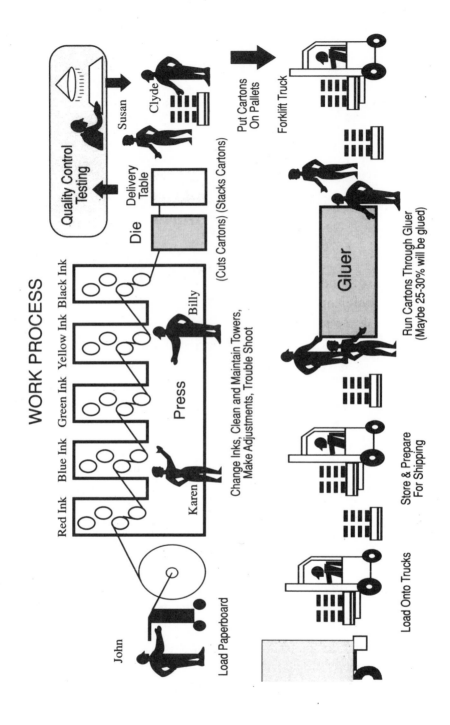

Quality Control Testing

Susan

Clyde

Delivery Table

Die

(Cuts Cartons) (Stacks Cartons)

Put Cartons On Pallets

Forklift Truck

Red Ink   Blue Ink   Green Ink   Yellow Ink   Black Ink

Press

Billy

Karen

Change Inks, Clean and Maintain Towers,
Make Adjustments, Trouble Shoot

John

Load Paperboard

Gluer

Run Cartons Through Gluer
(Maybe 25-30% will be glued)

Store & Prepare
For Shipping

Load Onto Trucks

Susan leaned over to Billy and said, "This is what I was worried about last week. I'll never be able to learn how to do all of this stuff."

"Don't worry," replied Billy. "We've got six weeks and we're going to get plenty of help. Besides, we're a team, remember?"

Boot camp wasn't far from the truth as far as Susan was concerned. Associates led the group step-by-step through tasks like loading the paperboard and operating the forklift before the trainees were allowed to practice. Susan found watching videos, like the one showing how the press was broken down, cleaned, and set up for a new run to be especially helpful, as well as the free time she spent in the plant as an observer. She lugged her "Bible" around and studied it faithfully, and Billy helped her when he could. His patient explanations cleared up many gray areas for her, but throughout it all she had a sinking feeling that six weeks wouldn't be long enough.

During a free session, Susan talked to Billy about some of the problems she was having.

"I passed the mechanical aptitude tests and I know they wouldn't have hired me if they didn't think I could do the job. But I'm really having a hard time. It seems so easy for you. What do you think I should do?"

Billy could tell Susan was really worried about not being able to keep up with the rest of the group. "So you're not as quick on some of these things. I had a hard time during the social skills training and you were a superstar. I think they allow for strengths and weaknesses here. I don't think you should worry, but let's ask the Assimilation Team."

That afternoon when the group had reassembled, Billy said, "Some of us are picking these skills up faster than others. Are we expected to master everything before we start working?"

"We don't expect you to remember all of these tasks until you've had more exposure to them. That's why we have the 'Bible' to refer to. We've also been monitoring individual performance over the last eight weeks. Part of our job is to make recommendations to the Jugglers about team composition. We need a balanced blend of technical and social skills on each team. In fact, tomorrow we'll be announcing your team assignments. So don't worry."

Susan smiled at Billy. "Thanks for everything," she said. "I hope we get on the same team, Billy. You've been such a patient coach. I wouldn't have made it this far without your help."

"You're more than welcome. Explaining things to you helps me to fix them more firmly in my own mind," Billy said. "You know, maybe we should ask if we could be assigned to the same team. When it comes to getting along with people, I see things a little more clearly after talking to you. I'd hate to lose that."

At the end of the day, Billy and Susan stopped Louis, Ken, and Sue on their way out the door.

Susan said, "Billy and I have sort of adopted each other as buddies during the training period. I helped him out in social skills and he's really been there for me throughout the technical training. Do you think we could be put on the same team?"

"We've noticed that you two work well together," Ken said. "It's up to the Jugglers to analyze the overall needs of all the teams and figure out how to mix the varying skills and personalities together. But we'll make your request known. I think it's a good idea."

Billy and Susan left that night anxiously awaiting tomorrow's assignments.

Chapter 5

▲▼▲▼

BECOMING A TEAM MEMBER

The next morning Dan, the rest of the Jugglers, and the Assimilation Team entered promptly at 8:00 to make the announcements.

Susan looked over at Billy and wagged her crossed fingers at him.

Dan kicked off the meeting. "It's been a long week for us. We have debated these team assignments at great length. In my opinion, they are the most important decisions that we managers have to make. The Assimilation Team has been invaluable in helping us pinpoint your strengths and weaknesses.

"Although these assignments are not cast in concrete, we have put a lot of time and thought into them. I hope that you'll give us the benefit of the doubt and give yourselves some time on your new team before requesting any changes. Without further conversation, let me show you your new teams."

Dan flipped on the overhead projector and revealed a chart listing the teams.

Susan grabbed Billy's arm excitedly. "Look Billy!" she said. "We're on the same team!"

"Alpha Team," Billy muttered. "I wonder what they'll be like." The noise in the room was so loud that Billy and Susan barely heard Dan shouting for silence. "You probably want to find out about your new team as soon as possible, so we've arranged for you to meet with them today before you start working next week."

The next slide Dan put up was a schedule of team meetings. Billy and Susan would meet with Alpha Team in one hour.

The members of Alpha Team were waiting for Billy and Susan in the small conference room.

"Good morning," said Susan, scanning the faces of her new associates. "I guess this is the time for you to check us out."

Two men and a woman stared back.

"That's right," the woman said. "I'm Karen. You must be Billy," she said to Susan. "And the big guy's Susan, right?" Her joke put everyone at ease.

Clyde, the older of the men, spoke up. "Karen's a cut up, but she's okay for a kid."

"I just got out of high school," Karen explained. "He thinks I'm still waiting for spring break. Maybe I am, a little," she admitted with a smile.

"I came here from another Clear Lake plant across the country," Clyde said. "It was a paper mill, though, so I didn't know anything about making cartons when I got here. We've all learned together, but we've only been at it for six months so we're still finding our way. It'll be good to have some new blood."

"I'm glad to hear you say that," said Billy, relaxing some. "To clear things up, my name is Billy," he said, looking pointedly at Karen, who grinned back. "I applied here after one too many layoffs from the automotive components plant where I worked. I ran five or six different machines in the shop there, so I think I'll catch on pretty fast."

"I might as well chime in here and tell you I'm not as comfortable with this machinery as Billy is," Susan said. "My last job was as a traffic and warehouse coordinator in a small retail distribution center. I needed strong communication skills for that. In fact I'm working on a degree in communication at a local college in my spare time. I just don't have a technical background to draw on. Billy helped me a lot during the training period. I hope you'll bear with me while I learn this."

"Don't worry about that," Karen said reassuringly. "John is our mechanical genius. As you see, he doesn't say much unless you ask him directly. But he can fix just about anything."

"I graduated a few years ago from the Technical Institute, certified as an electrical technician," John added. "Like Karen said, I can usually figure out what's going on with the machines. As for talking, well if it's important enough I'll speak up, but most of the time I am pretty quiet."

"By the way," Billy interjected, "you should know that my nickname is 'Bear,' because I act like one in the morning until I have my coffee."

"I can vouch for that," Susan said. "He really is a grouch in the morning."

The group spent some time getting to know each other. Clyde said he was thirty-eight, married with four kids. While he passed pictures, the others exchanged ages: Susan, thirty-one; Billy, thirty-four; John, twenty-four; and Karen, nineteen. Billy hauled out pictures of his two girls and Susan produced a snapshot of her three-year-old son. John said he didn't have pictures but that his sports car was his baby, and Karen told a lively story about her cats.

After a few minutes more of conversation, Clyde said, "We don't have much time today, so I suggest that we meet one hour every day next week and develop our mission statement, roles, and team guidelines."

"Don't you have those things already?" asked Billy.

Clyde replied, "We had some of it done. But since we've lost two members of the original team and run into trouble with some of the guidelines, I thought it might be a good idea to start over and develop better guidelines."

"What kind of trouble did you have?" Susan asked.

"One of the old members had a real attendance problem. Our guidelines were fairly loose. We finally had to start documenting all of his absences and late arrivals. He finally resigned last month. He was working two jobs and just couldn't deal with the rotating shift schedule and the meetings we had on overtime. So I think it's important that we get things straight up front."

"Before we go, let's decide whether we need to change our team name," Karen said. "What do you guys think about the name 'Alpha Team'?"

"Why did you call yourselves that in the first place?" Billy asked.

"You just said it," John said. "We want to be in first place and alpha is the first letter of the Greek alphabet."

"Why a Greek letter?" asked Susan.

"Because Athens was the birthplace of democracy," said John, "and we want to be a democratic team."

"I like it," said Susan. "How about if we put some words that stand for each letter of ALPHA, like Assertive Leaders, Productive Hardworking Achievers."

"Hey, that's a great idea!" said Karen.

"Watch out," said Billy. "This lady's dangerous when it comes to names, skits, and songs."

Monday was the team's first work day. After work they met to focus on a mission statement. They decided on the following mission:

> **ALPHA TEAM MISSION**
> To continually improve our ability to assertively lead and productively achieve higher levels of performance in quantity, quality, and teamwork.

Tuesday's meeting dealt with roles and responsibilities. Each member of the team was chosen to serve on a plant-wide team, most of which met once a week. Clyde was elected to continue on the Team Representative Council. Karen remained the Safety Representative. John kept his assignment on the Innovation Task Team, which reviewed technical improvements made on the presses. Susan was elected the new Quality Representative. And Billy was chosen to be on a task team that would form in several months to study press set-up and changeover time and find ways to speed them up.

Meetings on Wednesday, Thursday, and Friday were devoted to establishing team guidelines. In the end Alpha Team decided on nineteen guidelines falling under categories of behavior, attendance, meetings, breaks and lunches, cross-training, and interaction with other teams.

When that task was finished Billy said, "Although this is a good set of guidelines, what if something comes up that isn't covered?"

Clyde responded, "We'll deal with them as they arise. We can always add more guidelines later. And if there is something that keeps coming up and affects other teams, we

TEAM RESPONSIBILITIES

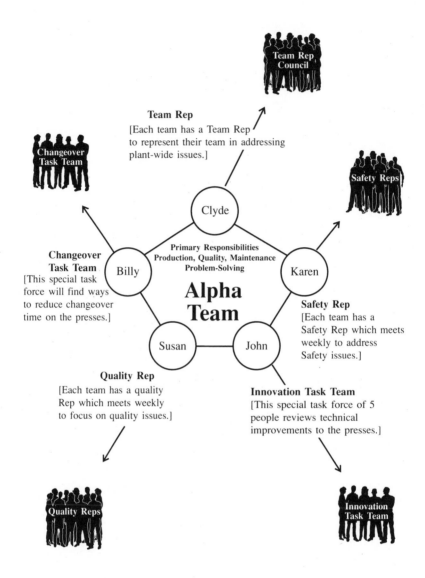

Team Rep Council

Team Rep
[Each team has a Team Rep to represent their team in addressing plant-wide issues.]

Changeover Task Team

Safety Reps

Changeover Task Team
[This special task force will find ways to reduce changeover time on the presses.]

Primary Responsibilities
Production, Quality, Maintenance
Problem-Solving

Alpha Team

Clyde

Billy

Karen

Susan

John

Safety Rep
[Each team has a Safety Rep which meets weekly to address Safety issues.]

Quality Rep
[Each team has a quality Rep which meets weekly to focus on quality issues.]

Innovation Task Team
[This special task force of 5 people reviews technical improvements to the presses.]

Quality Reps

Innovation Task Team

Note: Other task teams or project teams may be formed to deal with a variety of issues such as maintenance, assimilation of new hires, tool purchasing, etc.

can propose a policy for the plant which the teams' reps will then address."

"Well," said Susan, "I think we're off to a good start after one week on the job. I just hope everything keeps running this smoothly."

"Don't count on it," said John with a smile. "You're going to get plenty of experience solving new problems."

ALPHA TEAM GUIDELINES

TEAM BEHAVIOR:

— We will treat each other with respect.

— We will be direct and honest with each other.

— We will keep problems among our members within the team.

— If someone has a problem, we expect that member to let the appropriate people know.

— We will work together as a team.

ATTENDANCE:

— We expect all members to be on time every day.

— We will be at work at least ten minutes before the start of the shift to make smooth transitions.

— If we will be late, we will call and let the team know.

— If one of our members is absent, that member is responsible for getting someone to cover.

TEAM MEETINGS:

— We will have a team meeting at least once a week to review team rep, quality rep, safety rep, and task team meeting decisions and actions.

— We will rotate meeting leadership every week.

— Team meetings will be held off shift on Thursdays. Attendance is mandatory.

BREAKS & LUNCHES:

— We will stagger our breaks and lunches so that the press will continue running.

— Breaks will be taken at each member's discretion, provided that someone else is not on break.

— We will let each other know when we go on a break.

CROSS-TRAINING:

— We will cross-train each other over the next six months as time and opportunity allow.

— Cross-training will not take priority over meeting our production and quality goals.

DEALING WITH OTHER TEAMS:

— We will help other teams if requested.

— We will not meet our production and quality goals at the expense of the performance of other teams.

▲ Part II
▼ Storming

Chapter 6

▲▼▲▼

A LEADERSHIP STRUGGLE

As the first month went by, Billy became increasingly frustrated with the way things were going. His relationship with Clyde was tense. It seemed every time they got together, they wound up arguing. He decided to talk to Susan about it.

"I'm really tired of Clyde ordering me around. He acts like he's the supervisor just because he's a little bit older and the team rep. I'm getting fed up with it. What do you think I should do?"

Susan was sympathetic. "I know what you mean. It seems like since you and I are new to the team, we've got to do everything their way. I almost feel like we've got two teams instead of one."

"What are we going to do about it?" asked Billy.

"Well," said Susan, "we were taught in our training to address our problems with each other directly. We also have a team guideline that says whoever has the problem needs to talk to the appropriate people. So I think we should bring it up at the next team meeting."

"I'm going to let Clyde have it," fumed Billy. "If he thinks I'm going to just sit back and take orders, he's got another think coming."

"Now wait a minute," said Susan. "If you go in there and start yelling, it's going to make Clyde defensive and the situation is going to get worse. We've got two days before the meeting. Think about what you want to say and how you're going to say it. Don't go off half-cocked."

Billy calmed down a little bit and said, "Okay, I know you're right but I'm not used to doing this. You know, you're better at this sort of thing. Why don't you do the talking?"

"No, I won't," said Susan. "It's your issue with Clyde and you need to deal with it. What I will do is to start the discussion off and support you as we get into it."

Two days later at the meeting, Susan brought up the subject. "You know," she said, "Billy and I have been working on this team for a month now, but we don't really feel like full members yet."

"What do you mean?" asked Clyde.

"I'll tell you what she means," said Billy, losing his temper. "You keep ordering us around like you're the supervisor of this team and I'm getting sick of it!"

Clyde fired back. "Now look here. We've got some aggressive goals to meet. I don't expect you to know how to do everything yet, but when something goes wrong, you just stand around. Somebody has got to take charge and get things moving."

"I'm not just standing around," said Billy. "I'm trying to figure out what to do next."

"Well I know what to do next," said Clyde. "If you would just learn to take direction, everything would be okay."

"No, it won't be okay," said Susan. "I know we don't do everything as fast as you can, but we're learning. I think a lot of it is not so much what you say, but how you say it. When the press goes down, you get upset and start yelling at us."

"That's true, Clyde," said Karen. "I guess I've just gotten used to it."

"I'm only trying to get things running again as soon as possible," said Clyde defensively.

"Well, we all want that," said Billy.

"If you just tell us what to do, how are we going to learn to think for ourselves?" asked Susan.

John had been quiet up to this point. He held up his hand and said, "Hang on a minute. Let me say something. At first I was getting angry listening to Susan and Billy. I thought they were just complaining because they were frustrated with trying to learn the job.

"But the more I think about it, I can see what they're trying to say. Before they came on board, we had a certain way of doing things. When the press went down, we let Clyde take over and direct us because he seemed to know what to do the best. And I have to admit, I liked it that way because I didn't have to think about what to do. I could rely on Clyde.

"But Susan and Billy are right. We haven't really been open to other ideas. We've expected them to do things the way we've always done them. I can see how they might feel discounted. Let's make sure we really are a team."

The team got quiet for a minute. Karen broke the silence. "John, I think that's the most I've heard you say at one time."

The team laughed.

Clyde spoke again. "I guess maybe I do get a little heavy-handed sometimes."

"Hey, Clyde, I'm sorry I blew up at you," said Billy. "Now you know why they call me 'Bear.'"

"Okay," said John, "why don't we start with doing something different when the press goes down? What can we do?"

Billy replied, "Why don't we have a quick meeting at the front of the press and discuss why it went down and what we can do about it? Clyde can lead the meeting and help us learn what to do."

"Only if you promise to tell me when I get heavy-handed," said Clyde.

"Now we're getting somewhere," said Susan.

The next day Billy came over to Susan at lunch break. "I just wanted to thank you for getting me to talk about the situation with Clyde. It really made a big difference and I feel a lot better today."

"I think it did us all some good," said Susan. "I'm confident now that if we have a problem, we can talk about it and work it out."

Chapter 7

▲▼▲▼

AN UNFOCUSED TEAM
REPRESENTATIVE COUNCIL

Throughout Billy's and Susan's first month on the job, all ten teams at the plant revised their guidelines and operating procedures. Once this was done, a meeting of the team representatives was scheduled. Alpha Team met to decide what issues to put before the Team Representative Council.

Clyde explained the system to Susan and Billy. "Team reps deal with issues affecting the whole plant and with issues or concerns shared by more than one team.

"Before the new folks were hired, we started talking about the need for an attendance policy, because we had some people who were abusing the system. However, a couple of them left, so the issue lost some of its urgency."

"What are you going to address when you get back together this time?" asked Susan.

"That's what we're here to decide. Any suggestions?"

John spoke up. "I still think there should be a plant-wide policy on attendance. Though we're not having any problems right now, we had a big problem on our team three months ago. And I know of other teams where people are still taking advantage of the system—coming in later, calling in sick, and all that. It leaves teams short-handed and doesn't seem fair to the people who work hard every day."

"Does anyone else have an opinion on that?" asked Clyde.

"Sounds okay to me," said Susan.

Billy nodded in agreement. "I don't see how this place gets along without an attendance policy."

Clyde turned to Karen. "How about you, Karen?"

Karen had been late several times in the past few months and was absent more than anyone else.

Karen hedged. "I think what we've got is good enough, but I'll go along if that's what the team wants to do."

"Okay," said Clyde. "I'll get it on the agenda."

At the next Team Rep Council meeting, Craig, the team rep from the Jugglers, began the meeting.

"I'd like to welcome the six new reps to the group. After you've taken a minute to introduce yourselves, let's see what's on each team's list of issues to address."

There was a buzz of conversation as the reps got acquainted.

At the first lull, Bob, from the Press Wizards, spoke up. "The biggest problem right now is inconsistent quality standards from team to team. That should be our focus."

"I disagree," said Cathy, the representative from the Can Do Crew. "The most important issue right now is safety. We have a lot of new people around unfamiliar equipment and we need to ensure that good safety practices are followed."

George, the representative from Print Power, said, "Right now our first priority should be establishing a baseline of acceptable behavior so that everyone has consistent guide-lines to follow. We know that attendance has been a real issue over the last three months. Let's develop a policy that is uniform so we don't have the problem again."

"I agree," said Clyde, seeing his opportunity. "Alpha Team also believes that a plant-wide attendance policy is warranted. There are too many team-to-team differences on handling attendance problems."

"That's all true," said Kent, the team rep from the Gluing Go-Getters, "but my team says that improving production and on-time delivery performance is what's needed most. The biggest obstacle right now is slow changeovers and, as you know, changeover time is our biggest source of down-time."

"We think so, too," said Mary, from the Customer Service Crusaders. "Whatever else we do, we should focus on improving customer satisfaction."

The discussion continued for about fifteen minutes, with several heated exchanges about priorities. Finally, Craig held up his hand.

"Since there is such a wide difference of opinion on what to tackle first, I suggest that we develop some guidelines on setting priorities."

The council spent the next two hours defining their mission, responsibilities, and guidelines for identifying topics to address.

After they had completed their initial guidelines, Craig said, "According to our criteria, all of the issues introduced earlier belong to some other group except one—the issue of attendance."

"Inconsistent quality standards should be addressed by the Quality Reps. Safety issues should be addressed by the Safety Reps. The press changeover time issue will be ad-dressed by the new task team scheduled to start in a couple

TEAM REP MISSION

To initiate and support continuous improvement of high performance at Clear Lake.

RESPONSIBILITIES

COMMUNICATION & COOPERATION

— Understand what other teams are doing.

— Act as a communication link to other committees & task teams.

— Represent the views of our teams.

— Ensure effective transitions.

— Improve morale and job satisfaction.

— Stay up-to-date on business status.

— Delegate issues & support the work of other teams.

DECISION MAKING & PROBLEM SOLVING:

— Identify issues to address.

— Delegate issues to appropriate teams or keep them.

— Solicit input, gather data, & develop options.

— Make decisions & recommendations when appropriate.

— Facilitate implementation.

ADMINISTRATION:

— Coordinate & prioritize resource allocations.

— Coordinate cross-training.

— Organize & document our work.

— Help with specific administrative duties when requested.

— Coordinate overtime.

— Coordinate attendance.

GUIDELINES FOR IDENTIFYING TOPICS

CRITERIA FOR TOPICS:

— The issue deals with our values & beliefs.

— The issue falls into one of the following categories: Business Peformance, Customer Service, Technical Environment, or Policy.

— The issue affects more than one team.

— A majority of the team reps support discussing it.

— The issue is not being addressed by another group or task team.

— The issue is submitted in writing to the Council with appropriate background material and suggestions, using the established form.

of months. So that leaves attendance for us. I suggest we start there next week."

The group agreed to get input from each team on guidelines for a plant-wide attendance policy and address the issue at their next meeting.

When the Team Rep Council met the following week to debate the attendance policy, opinions varied on how the policy should be written.

Some of the group felt the policy should be very specific leaving little room for interpretation. Others felt the policy should only provide a general outline, with the details left for each team to decide.

The group finally reached a consensus on the key points and wording of the policy. After writing the policy, they reported back to their teams.

Chapter 8

▲▼▲▼

ATTENDANCE PROBLEMS

At the weekly meeting of Alpha Team, Clyde distributed copies of the attendance policy for the team to review.

ATTENDANCE POLICY

During a six-month period, if you have three occurrences which are not supported by your team and which your team has documented, the following guidelines will apply:

1. Occurrence #4 = No pay for the absence.
2. Occurrence #5 = No pay & a two-day suspension.
3. Occurrence #6 = Recommendation for termination.

(Three "tardies" will count as one occurrence.)

"Any questions?" asked Clyde.

"If someone is just five or ten minutes late, do we document that?" asked Susan.

"Well, that's up to the team as usual," said Clyde. "I guess we need to establish our own guidelines on enforcing this policy."

John spoke up. "I think we need to be fairly strict about this. Before Susan and Billy were hired we had a real problem on this team with one member. We didn't really deal with it for the first month and I think that made it worse. It became okay to be ten or fifteen minutes late. We let the problem drag out too long and just avoided addressing it until it became a crisis."

Clyde turned to Karen who was looking uncomfortable. "You know if we'd had this policy over the last two months and documented all the times you've been tardy or absent, you'd be in serious trouble right now."

"I didn't know how to bring it up, but it's really bothered me that you've missed a couple of days without letting us know," Susan said. And you're late at least one day a week."

"This is just what I'm talking about," said John. "Some bad feelings are already beginning to develop over this. I like you, Karen, but we have got to set some standards and maintain them, or the whole team will begin to suffer for it."

"It's not about liking you. We all like you. I like my son, but I still make rules so that we both know what to expect," Susan said.

"Okay," said Clyde, "How about this? If you're less than five minutes late and have a reasonable explanation, we'll talk about it. If it happens more than once in the same week or if you're more than five minutes late, we will document it."

"That's a little lenient," said John. "Our team guidelines say we're to be here ten minutes before the start of the shift, so five minutes is really fifteen minutes late. But I guess I'm willing to try it for a while and see how it goes."

The other members agreed to Clyde's suggestion. The team decided not to write the guideline down and publish it, because they wanted to remain flexible.

Karen was absent the following Tuesday.

"Maybe there's something wrong with her that she hasn't told us about," said Susan.

"She could have at least called in to let us know she wouldn't be here," John said angrily.

Billy frowned. "I don't like doing this, but I guess we should document it."

"How about we just write it up for now. We can talk to Karen when she comes back and see if she has a good reason before we document it," Susan suggested.

When Karen showed up the next day, the team confronted her.

"We were irritated that you didn't call us yesterday," John said. "Why were you absent?"

"I just didn't feel good yesterday," Karen said defensively.

"Well, why didn't you call and let us know?" asked Susan, hoping there would be a good reason.

"I meant to," Karen said, "but I just forgot. I'm sorry. It won't happen again," she muttered, avoiding eye contact.

"I'm glad to hear you say that, but we still have to document this and put it in your file," said Clyde.

He handed her the form which the others had already signed. Karen quickly scribbled her name across the bottom, eager to get away from the group and her own uncomfortable feelings. "I really am going to do better," she said. "You'll see."

The team left. Susan touched Karen on the arm after the others had gone. "Is everything all right really?" she asked. "Are you unhappy with your job?"

"Oh no," Karen assured her. "I love working here with all of you. It's the best part of my life."

Susan looked at her co-worker's unhappy eyes. She felt helpless, but made one last offer. "Karen, please come to me if I can do anything to help you. I really care about you."

Over the next two weeks, Karen was absent again without telling the team and was late four times, although only two of them were more than five minutes late. The team documented the absence and two tardies.

At the next team meeting, John brought up the subject of her attendance. "Karen, you are really getting into a danger zone with your attendance and your performance in general over the last two months has been erratic. You've been tired, you've made a lot of mistakes, and you've had a couple of close calls in safety. Is something wrong?"

"No, nothing is wrong, " Karen said loudly. "I've just been a little under the weather."

"Maybe you should go see a doctor," suggested Susan.

"I don't need a doctor," Karen said. "I can take care of myself."

▲▼▲▼

The next day Susan talked to Billy during the break. "You see, something is wrong with Karen. But whatever is going on, she's determined to keep us out."

"I'll tell you this," said Billy. "I saw her Saturday night when I was at the mall with my family. She was running with a pretty rough crowd and she looked like she'd been drinking quite a bit."

"Did you talk to her?" asked Susan.

"No, I didn't," said Billy. "She was across the mall."

Later, as Billy was walking down the back side of the press, he saw Karen put her hand in a dangerous position.

He yelled across the press. "Karen, get your hand out of there!"

But it was too late. Karen screamed and yanked her hand back. Blood was streaming down her arm. Billy hit the emergency stop button on the press and ran to her. She was shaking all over and blood continued to flow from her hand.

"Hang on," said Billy. "Everything is going to be okay. Let me take a look at it."

It was a deep cut but all of her fingers were still intact. "Let's get you to the emergency room," said Billy.

Billy went with Karen to the hospital. He came back a couple of hours later and reported to the team.

"It's serious but she'll be okay. It looks like she's going to be out of work for a while, though."

"She knows better than to put her hand in the press like that," John said.

"Something is wrong with her," said Clyde. "We've all seen it over the last two months and we're lucky something more serious hasn't happened. Whatever is wrong, we need to confront her when she gets back and deal with it."

Two days later Karen called and asked to meet with the team at 3:00 that afternoon. At 3:30 the team was still waiting in the small conference room.

"We've been waiting thirty minutes," said Billy angrily. "Where is she?"

"She's been in Dan's office with the door closed for the last hour and a half," said Susan. "She'll be in when they get through talking. Just calm down, Billy."

"Okay," Billy said. "But what are we going to say when she gets in here?"

"Why don't we just listen to her and take it from there?" said Susan.

Ten minutes later, Karen and Dan came into the room. Karen looked upset. They sat down and she said, "The doctor says I'll be out of work for about six weeks because of my hand. She says it will heal, but it was a close call. I almost lost two fingers."

"I'm just glad it wasn't worse," said Susan, trying to be supportive.

Karen looked tearful. She started to say something, then stopped. The team waited.

Dan said, "Karen has something else she needs to tell you."

When Karen finally spoke, her voice was thick with tears. "During the next six weeks, I'll also be entering a drug and alcohol rehabilitation program. I have a problem and I need some help. I guess I really didn't want to admit it to myself, but this accident really scared me.

"I also want to apologize for the trouble I've caused the team lately. I really do value this job and all of you. All the cards you sent me were wonderful, but they made me feel guilty, too, because I know I've let you down. I just hope all of you will be willing to take me back when I return. "

The team was quiet for a moment until Billy said, "You do what you need to do and we'll be waiting for you when you get back. Right guys?" he asked the other three.

"Right," they echoed.

Karen left the room looking much happier than when she came in.

The rest of the team stayed for a few more minutes to discuss the situation.

"I knew something was wrong," said Susan. "I should have pushed harder to get her to talk."

"There's no sense blaming yourself," said John. "It's her problem and she's facing it."

"Well, this leaves us with a problem," said Clyde. "We're down to four members for the next six weeks. What should we do about it?"

"Didn't you run with four people for a while before Susan and I got here?" asked Billy.

"Yes, we did," said Clyde. "It was a little rough, but we managed."

"Let's try it again," said Susan. "Billy and I have had enough experience now that I think we can manage. We can ask other teams to help us for an hour or two when we have problems or when one of us has a meeting."

"That's okay by me," said John. "But be prepared. It'll be tough getting help when we need it."

▲ Part III
▼ Norming

Chapter 9

▲▼▲▼

MAKING SMOOTH SHIFT TRANSITIONS

John's prediction proved to be true. The next week was a difficult one for the team. Whenever one of them had a meeting to attend, Alpha Team had trouble getting coverage from another team. The Alpha Team had to shut the press down during lunch breaks. It also seemed to have more than its regular share of problems. The group discussed the dilemma at the team meeting that week.

"Our performance has really slipped this week," said Clyde. "Production and quality performance are both down and they aren't getting any better."

"I didn't realize it would be this hard adjusting to a four-person team," said Susan. "If the other teams would just help out when we asked them, things would certainly go a lot smoother."

"I'm getting tired of asking them," Billy said. "Every time we ask for help we get a different excuse—they're too busy, or someone is at a meeting, or they've run into some problem and need their whole team to fix it."

"Why can't we just get one person assigned to our team until Karen comes back?" asked Susan.

"Because that would leave some other team short-handed," replied John.

"Well, what are we going to do?" asked Billy.

"I don't know," said Clyde. "But I might as well tell you some more bad news. I just got a complaint from the Press Wizards about how we're leaving the press when we turn it over to them. They say our housekeeping is poor and that they have to replenish most of the supplies before they can begin work. They want to have a meeting with us to discuss it. I've got one arranged at the end of the shift today."

"Well, what do they expect?" fumed Billy. "They know we don't have a full team right now."

"One guy said he thought we were trying to make our numbers look good at their expense," Clyde said.

"Just wait," Billy said angrily. "I've got a few things to tell them."

"Now hang on, Bear," said Susan. "Stop your growling and get those claws in. If we handle things right, maybe some good can come out of this."

"Okay," said Billy, doubtfully. "I'll try."

That afternoon Alpha Team and the Press Wizards met to discuss the situation. Bob, the team rep from the Press Wizards, spoke first.

"We called this meeting to discuss ways to make shift transitions smoother. Over the past week, several things have not been done when we arrived at the beginning of our shift. We've had to clean up after you and replenish most of the supplies before we could start working. It's taking an extra thirty minutes before we can really get going."

Another member of the Press Wizards jumped in. "Are you guys trying make us look bad?"

That comment really made Billy angry. "Listen, you guys aren't perfect either. We've heard some comments from the team you pass off to and they say you leave them with a mess, too. So don't get so high and mighty about it!"

Susan put a restraining hand on Billy's arm. "Okay, cool off, guys. Let's talk calmly about the problem and focus on finding solutions.

"As you all know," she continued, "we're down to four members for the next six weeks and we're struggling to adapt to the situation. It's true that our housekeeping is not up to our usual standards. We're certainly not trying to make your team look bad. We've just had to let a few things slide, and housekeeping has been one of them."

Another member of the Press Wizards commented, "You're not the first team in the plant to operate with four members. Other teams have done it, too."

"I know they have," said Susan. "And we're getting it together. But we need you to help us instead of attacking us. Remember, we're all in this together."

"She's right," said Bob. "I guess we have been trying to blame you instead of looking for ways to help. What can we do to make things better for all of us?"

"For one thing," said John, "we could draw up a checklist of everything that needs to be done before we turn the press over to you. When you get here, you can go down the checklist and see what hasn't been done. I'll agree to stay over on your shift and keep working until everything on the list is finished."

"That's a good idea," said Bob. "But I think we can do more than that. How about if one of the Press Wizards comes in two hours early every day to help out?" Bob asked his team.

When the Press Wizards agreed, Clyde said gratefully, "That would be a tremendous help. Maybe if we ask them, one of the Can Do Crew would stay a couple hours over. That would give us five people for half of the shift. We should be able to handle it ourselves for the other four hours."

The two teams agreed and worked up a shift transition checklist. Clyde said he would talk to the Can Do Crew's team rep the next day and work out an agreement with them.

As the meeting broke up, Billy approached Susan. "You were right again. Not only have we eased our problems for the next six weeks, but we've also improved our relationship with the Press Wizards. I really admire the way that you avoid all the bull and get right to the heart of the matter."

"Thanks, Billy. It's amazing what can be accomplished if we go into a situation with the right attitude. I just hope the quality reps can achieve as much as we did today."

Chapter 10

▲▼▲▼

ADDRESSING QUALITY ISSUES

The following week Susan attended the regular weekly meeting of the quality reps. Like Susan, half of the group was new to the plant. They had been arguing about the most effective way to improve quality for a month.

Annette, the representative from the Jugglers, began the discussion. "So far, all we've managed to agree on is that we disagree. Today let's see if we can develop some methods to identify and address quality problems as they arise.

"Here's what we know: Each team is responsible for its own quality control. During a production run, samples are checked frequently. If bad cartons keep coming through, we hold onto those samples and talk about them in our quality meetings. We also examine and discuss any cartons that are returned by our customers.

"Our main concern has been that quality standards vary from team to team. Cartons that one team may scrap are viewed as acceptable by another team and passed on to the customer. Although we have statistical process control procedures, there is still too much variation between teams on what is considered a good carton. We need to set a standard and figure out how to maintain consistency.

"Perhaps the best way to begin is to identify the problems that exist, analyze the causes, and develop some possible solutions before we come up with an action plan. Any ideas?"

Susan raised her hand. "Customer returns are way too high. If our mission as a plant is to produce superior products, then we shouldn't have any cartons returned. They should be made right the first time with zero defects."

"That's fine in theory," said Tim, from Print Power, "but there is no such thing as a perfect carton. There will always be variation in color and minor defects that are barely detectable. Our main problem is that quality control is still largely subjective, relying on individual judgment. That's why some teams are throwing away good cartons and some teams are letting unacceptable cartons get through."

"I think it's a question of not following procedures," said Betty, from the Press Wizards. "Although the system's not foolproof, if everyone followed the procedures we do have, we could reduce our returns dramatically."

Annette summarized. "Okay, customer returns are too high, quality control is too dependent on individual judgment, and procedures are not being followed consistently. What are the causes?"

David, from the Can Do Crew, spoke up. "If you ask me, customer requirements are just not specific enough. There's no clear guideline on what they will accept. I think they have the same problem we do. Different people at their plant may accept or reject the same carton, depending on who's looking at it."

"About subjective judgments," said Susan, "I think new associates judge quality more harshly than the people who have been here longer."

"I agree," said Tim. "The new people tend to throw away cartons with any flaw, not realizing that slight imperfections may be acceptable to the customer. They are overly cautious and that makes the scrap rate go up needlessly. They don't realize that we could shut the press down for hours and still not erase those minor blemishes."

"As for not following procedures," Betty said, "I think there are two main causes. First, there isn't enough time to make the appropriate checks and, second, the new people haven't been trained sufficiently."

The group debated other potential causes and argued about the merits of various opinions. Annette finally interrupted the debate.

"Part of our problem is that we don't have data that shows what's really happening. What's the leading source of scrap?" she asked the group. A chorus of answers rang out.

"Color variation."

"Missing print."

"Jagged cuts."

"Well," said Annette, "first let's collect some data and make a chart of the leading sources of defects. That will tell us where to start."

The group agreed to chart the quantity and sources of scrap for each run of the press. They quickly identified the categories to track.

"While we're gathering data," said Annette, "what else can we do?"

"Establish clear customer requirements," said Tim. "Let's work with the customers to set up a 'defect book' that illustrates the various problems and outlines what is acceptable. I'll take responsibility for that one and work with the Can Do Crew to set up appointments with every customer."

"Let's get some refresher training going," said Betty. "I'll set up a schedule for each team to get a two-hour review of the standard procedures."

"That still doesn't guarantee that people will follow the procedures," Susan said. "We need a way to pinpoint what each team is doing."

"I know!" said David. "The team reps can sign a tag on each pallet every time they complete a run. Then we'll have a way to trace customer returns back to the team that produced the cartons. We can also track how much scrap each team is producing. Then we'll have enough data to see which teams are letting scrap get by and which teams are tossing too much."

"Okay," said Annette, "let's get to work!"

Susan reported the results of the meeting back to her team. "So there are some new things we need to start doing," she said. "First, we need to start tracking scrap data. Second, we need to sign every pallet we approve. Third, we need to sign up for a time to go through quality training again and review procedures. And when we get the new 'defect books' developed, each team will get a copy to keep on the press."

"It sounds good to me," said Clyde. "I'm all for more consistency between teams. At least this way we'll know which teams are causing customer returns and generating the most scrap."

"I'm not sure I like this," Billy said nervously. "Where I used to work, the supervisors would use this kind of information as an excuse to come down on us."

"Self-managing doesn't mean we aren't accountable for what we do," said John. "You've got to trust that people will deal with the facts and handle the situation in a constructive way."

"Who's to say that all of the teams will follow these suggestions?" asked Billy.

"There are no guarantees," said Susan. "Each team has got to be committed to making this work. But I know the quality reps are determined to make improvements and we'll chart our progress at each meeting. Let's just be sure Alpha Team does our part."

"Okay," said Billy, reluctantly. "I guess part of the reason I'm hesitant about this is that I'm not a rep and I haven't seen these groups in action."

Clyde patted his shoulder. "You're going to get your chance next week, buddy. The Press Changeover Task Team has scheduled its first meeting and you're our delegate, remember?"

"That's right," said Billy, in surprise. "I'd forgotten about that. I just hope I fit in. It's not easy to negotiate with a bear," he joked.

"Hey, Bear, you've learned more about how the press works in less time than just about anybody in the plant. You're twice as fast as any of us during a press changeover. So just pay attention and speak up when you've got something to contribute," John said reassuringly.

"Thanks, John," Billy said gruffly. He felt a warm glow of pride. "I'm not used to so much praise."

"And don't worry, we'll remind you of your manners," Susan said.

Chapter 11

▲▼▲▼

ACCELERATING PRESS CHANGEOVER

Billy went to his first meeting of the new Press Changeover Task Team. There were four other representatives, including William from the Jugglers, who began the meeting.

"Thank you all for signing up for this task team. Long press changeover times are our major cause of press downtime. Some of the changeovers are taking up to five or six hours. It's just taking too long to clean the press, change the inks, reset the press, and get started again. If we can figure out ways to significantly reduce changeover time, it will increase plant productivity dramatically. It will also allow us to make shorter production runs more often, which will improve our ability to respond to the customer."

"If everyone would just work faster, we could cut the time down a lot," Billy said.

"That's true," said William, nodding. "But not everyone has that sense of urgency or even the ability to work so fast. I think we need to find ways to simplify changeovers so we can work smarter as well as harder to get the job done."

"Where do we begin?" asked Elliot, another member of the task team.

"Let's define our mission," William said. "What is it we're trying to accomplish?"

"Well, changeovers need to be done fast," said Billy.

"Right. What else?" he asked.

"They need to be done right the first time, " said Elliot.

"They need to be done in a safe way," said Jane. "We have a high percentage of accidents during changeovers."

"There should also be a set of procedures that are easy to explain and remember," added William.

"I've got it!" said Billy. "We can be the F.A.S.T. Team and our mission can be to develop a F.A.S.T. (Fast, Accurate, Safe, Trainable) method to reduce changeover time."

"That's great!" said Elliot. "How'd you do that?"

"I picked it up by watching Susan on our team. I didn't think I was good at it, but I guess I must have soaked up more from her than I thought."

"Okay," said William. "It looks like we've got our name and our mission statement. Now let's define the scope of our activities. What should we investigate? Let's make a list up on the flip chart."

The team brainstormed a list of issues that included the sequence of events, mechanical problems, operating procedures, tools, materials, communication, and attitudes.

"That's a lot to investigate at once," said Jane. "Where do we start?"

"I have an idea," said Billy. "We could videotape a normal changeover and then analyze the tape to look for ways to improve. My high school football coach did that. Then we could watch ourselves in games and practice and see our actions and errors more objectively."

"It is a good idea," said Elliot, "but wouldn't the team that's being filmed get nervous or work faster because they are on camera?"

"Maybe, but that shouldn't matter," Carl said. "We can even film several teams doing a changeover for perspective."

"I'd be willing to ask my team to be guinea pigs," Billy added. "I'm sure they would say yes."

"Okay," said William. "Let's try it. If Alpha Team agrees, we'll pick a time next week and tape a changeover. Then we can begin studying the tape at our next meeting."

William filmed Alpha Team during a changeover two days later. When the F.A.S.T. Team met the following week, they settled in to watch the tape.

"What should we be looking for as we watch this?" asked Jane.

"First, we should record and time each step," said William. "Then we can add up where most of the time is going and focus our energies there."

"I'm sure we're going to get ideas just watching it," said Billy. "We can keep track of all of the thoughts and suggestions we have along the way and discuss them later."

For the next three meetings, the team studied the videotape, writing down the time spent on various steps of the changeover and coming up with ideas for improvement. When they finished the tape they made a chart of the biggest users of time and discussed their causes.

After several more meetings, they had developed a list of fifty suggestions for improvement, including cleaning new rollers ahead of time, having replacement inks near the press, and building portable changeover tool trays with all the tools needed to do a changeover.

"I think we've got some great ideas here that will benefit everyone in the plant," William said.

"Now how are we going to get people to try them?" asked Lou. "Each team has developed its own system of doing changeovers. It may be hard to convince them to try our suggestions."

Elliot said, "Let's write up our suggestions and present them at the next general plant meeting. Then we can see how the teams respond."

"At the same time," said Billy, "we can implement these suggestions on our own teams to show how well they work. That will take care of four teams. When the other teams see how we've cut changeover time, surely they'll want to do it, too."

The F.A.S.T. Team made a presentation the following week at a general plant meeting. They also applied their recommendations to their own teams and found them successful. But despite their commitment, the other teams didn't respond.

F.A.S.T. Team met to talk about the problem.

"Why won't they try some of these suggestions?" Jane was frustrated. "The downtime reports and the changeover time for our four teams is down by almost fifty percent. It's obvious that we're doing something right."

William replied, "Remember, we've been working on this for more than six weeks. You've had time to think about the problems and develop your own solutions. The other teams haven't had that opportunity. All they saw was this team making a presentation of fifty suggestions. They don't feel any ownership of the solutions. Maybe we need to come up with another strategy for convincing them to try some of these suggestions for themselves."

"I see what you mean," Billy said. "At first I didn't want to listen to some of the suggestions that the quality reps made." Billy paused, thinking, before adding, "How about this? Since we represent all three shifts, let's offer to help another team out during changeover. If necessary, one of their members can fill in on our teams. Then they can see firsthand what we're talking about. We might even get suggestions from them to reduce changeover time even more."

The F.A.S.T. Team members did offer to help other teams during changeovers. Billy spent extra time helping each of the F.A.S.T. Team members improve their own changeover times. More and more the team began to view him as an expert in changeover procedures.

Within two weeks practically every team had adopted at least half of the fifty suggestions and come up with more ideas for improvement.

"Downtime reports show that changeover time has dropped for every team and is decreasing every week. This team deserves congratulations for a job well done," said William.

"Does this mean we're out of business?" asked Billy.

"Before we stop," said Tom, "let's document the amount of time that has been saved during changeovers and show folks the impact it will have in productivity and our gainsharing checks. That might give everyone even more incentive for continuing the effort."

"That's a good idea," said William. "I'll work with the accounting people and see if we can generate some numbers. Then this team can make a final presentation at the next general plant meeting."

"I think Billy ought to have the honors," said Elliot. "He's made the biggest contribution to this team so he should report the good news."

The rest of the team agreed heartily.

Billy was embarrassed by the attention, but he left the meeting feeling proud that he had made an important contribution to the plant.

Billy gave the presentation on productivity improvement to the rest of the plant. All the associates applauded the work of the F.A.S.T. Team and the contribution it had made.

And Billy noticed another result of his work on the task team. He was becoming an informal leader in the plant. His co-workers were turning to him for help and guidance.

▲ Part IV
▼ Performing

Chapter 12

▲▼▲▼

CROSS-TRAINING IN ACTION

When Alpha Team gathered Thursday for their weekly meeting, Clyde reported on the previous Team Rep Council discussion.

"The last couple of months have really been busy. Teams have focused on quality-related activities and changeover improvements. However, the team reps are concerned that cross-training has fallen by the wayside. Our team's initial guidelines said that we would be cross-trained within six months, and we're not even close to meeting that goal."

John responded, "We also said in our guidelines that cross-training would not take priority over meeting production and quality goals. And since we've been a four-person team lately, we haven't had the flexibility for cross-training."

Billy said, "I've really been consumed by the changeover task team and helping to get our suggestions implemented. However, that's winding down now and I should have more time available."

Susan said, "I've been busy with helping to get the new 'defect books' put together, but I agree that we need to refocus. By the way, I talked to Karen yesterday and she said she'll be coming back to work next week."

"Great! We can sure use her. How's she doing?" asked Billy.

"She says she's doing great and is looking forward to coming back to work," replied Susan. "She's a little anxious about catching up on what she missed, but I told her not to worry about it."

"Why don't we wait until she gets here and have our discussion about cross-training then," Clyde suggested. "That would be a good time to bring her up to speed on what's been happening and talk about what to do next."

Karen returned the following week and the team scheduled a special meeting to welcome her back. She hugged everyone and said, "It's really great to be back. My hand is back to normal and my treatment at the rehabilitation center was excellent. Thanks, Billy, for dropping in to check on me. And thanks, Susan and John, for the calls. Clyde, you get an extra hug for that sweet card. It was a lot easier to get better knowing I had you people to come back to."

The team summarized what had been happening over the last couple months, focusing on the changes in quality and changeover activities.

Karen looked at the team in amazement. "Wow! You guys have really been busy. I knew I'd have some catching up to do, but I didn't know it would be so much."

"Don't worry," said Billy. "I'll show you what to do during changeovers, and Susan can take you through the new quality procedures. It won't take you long to pick them up."

"It'll be a piece of cake," Susan reassured her.

"Well," said Clyde, getting back to business, "where do we go from here? We said we'd focus on cross-training when Karen got back. I need to let the team reps know our plans."

"Let's start by identifying what everyone is good at now," said John. "Then let's identify our weaknesses and go from there."

The team made a list of the twenty critical skill areas required to run the press. Beside each skill they noted whether each team member was at the beginner, intermediate, or advanced level. When they had finished, Susan said, "We know more than I realized."

"Yes," said John. "But there are still a number of areas where only one of us is really advanced. I think we should focus on those skills first and make sure we have a back-up on our team for each area."

They then determined who wanted to be trained for those skills and who would do the training.

"There are too many things to learn all at once," said Billy. "How about making a work schedule where each of us spends time paired up with the expert on our team. Then we can see how long this is going to take."

They worked on the schedule and decided that they could cross-train at least one back-up to be their "expert" in all twenty skill areas within three months.

"This looks good," said Clyde. "I'll report our plan back to the team reps."

Over the next three months, Alpha Team made excellent progress. Their production and quality performance continued to improve, and they continued to cross-train each other.

During this time, the Jugglers established a weekly "Production Huddle" with each team to review their weekly results and talk about what was going well and how to address problems. William was the Juggler member responsible for the Huddle.

"The performance improvement has really been great on this team," he said at one of the Huddles. "Production is up, scrap is down, cross-training is progressing, downtime is minimum, and you seem to work out problems with very little fuss. What's your secret?"

Susan looked at Karen. "We all wondered whether we could have prevented Karen's accident by speaking up sooner. Since then, I think we've all been committed to really communicating with each other and dealing with things when they first arise instead of waiting for them to become a crisis."

"We also are careful about documenting and tracking our performance," said John, "We have a checklist for just about everything we do to make sure things get done right and we know on a daily basis where we stand on all of our key performance indicators like production output, scrap rate, and press downtime."

"In addition, we've also tried to balance the workload," said Billy. "Matching each task with the person or persons who do them the best works well for us."

"Well, it's impressive," said William. "I wish all the teams were improving at your pace. Is there anything that you're concerned about?"

"I'm a little bothered by the relationships between teams," said Billy. "We've been so intent on our own team's performance lately that we seem to have forgotten we're a part of the whole plant. We never even see some teams because they're on other shifts. I don't even know some of the associates. We need something to bring us all together."

"That's a good point, Billy," said William. "Others have made the same comment. I'll bring it up at the next meeting of the Jugglers and see what we can do about it."

Chapter 13

▲▼▲▼

THE "EVENT"— ORGANIZATIONAL MESHING

William mentioned Billy's idea to the Jugglers at the next meeting. "I think Billy is right. We've lost sight of the big picture. In spite of the Team Rep Council and our common goals, I think the groups still feel separate from each other. We need something to get everyone on one big team so that we can truly focus on issues that face the whole plant," he concluded.

"Yeah," said Craig. "Some kind of event that gets everyone in the same room at the same time."

"Let's do it," said Dan, slapping the table for emphasis. "Next month will be relatively slow. Let's find a few days we can shut the plant down and bring everyone together. Since we've just turned the corner financially, we can also use this time to celebrate our success."

Dan called in consultants who worked with the Jugglers to organize physical activities and outdoor problem-solving challenges. They developed a series of games, exercises and discussions about team building, team-to-team relationships, and feedback.

When the announcement went out to the teams telling them to plan for 'The Big Event,' Alpha Team discussed it at its weekly meeting.

"What the heck is this?" asked Billy.

"I don't know," said Clyde. "The Jugglers are being secretive about it. All they said was dress casually and wear sneakers."

"Will everyone be there?" asked Karen.

"Yes," replied Clyde. "The plant will be closed the whole three days and all sixty-five of us will meet at the community center."

"Wow," said Karen. "Spring break is finally here!"

On the first morning of the event, the community meeting hall was buzzing with chatter. Dan went up front and held up his hands for silence. "We have an exciting three days ahead of us. The themes that we will address will include Awareness, Choice, Trust, and Accountability. We have a variety of experiences lined up to help all of us look at ourselves and each other from a new angle. We've also worked in a little celebration of our financial gains. Now let's have some fun."

Dan turned the program over to the trainers. For the next two days Clear Lake associates explored differences between teams, conflicts between the three shifts, and team-building experiences.

They played "The Electric Fence" game in which groups had to get their members through an imaginary electric fence without "getting zapped." In the "Trust Walk" people were blindfolded and led through the park. They built a computer made of people and discovered which buttons to push to access information, analyze it, and solve problems. They participated in plant-wide discussions about conflicts between and within teams. They identified all they'd accomplished in the first two years of operation and pinpointed the challenges ahead.

On the third day, Dan faced the group and said, "We've had a great time so far, but we've saved the best for last. While we were meeting yesterday our consultants built a fifteen-foot wall back at the plant. Our job is to figure out how to get over it. So everybody get in your cars and meet at the plant in thirty minutes."

Alpha Team rode to the plant in Clyde's station wagon. When everyone had arrived, one of the trainers climbed on top of the wooden wall they had built and gave the group the rules.

"You have one hour to get everyone to the top of this wall and then climb down the ladder to the other side. You can have only three people on the platform at the top of the wall at one time, and you've got to rotate so that no one person helps lift up more than five people. Think carefully about how to use your resources, and don't forget that the last couple of people have got a tough job."

Everyone gathered around at the bottom of the wall to plot a strategy and decide who should go over first. Billy volunteered to go last because he was good at climbing. "I'll be fine if someone will dangle their feet and let me grab hold. Whoever it is, though, just make sure your ankles are screwed on," he said.

After several minutes of planning, they began hoisting people up and pulling them over the wall. As each person reached the top, the crowd let out a cheer.

Finally Billy was the only person left. John hung from the top and was held steady by two others. Billy jumped up and grabbed John's ankles and slowly pulled himself up. Halfway up, he grabbed John's belt and when it snapped John's pants started to slide down. The crowd hooted, "Take 'em off!"

John managed to keep his pants on and he and Billy finally made it to the top. Everyone cheered and tangled themselves up in a group hug. They had finished with twenty minutes to spare.

Each person signed the wall, which would remain on the plant grounds to commemorate their experience. Before he dismissed everyone, Dan passed out gainsharing checks to celebrate the plant's success.

"This has been a great experience for me," he said emotionally. "It really shows what we can do when we all pull together."

On the way home, Alpha Team stopped for pizza. "That was amazing," Susan said, licking sauce from her fingers, hungrily.

"I really feel connected to everyone at the plant now," Karen added.

"I'm just glad I didn't lose my pants," John said in relief.

Chapter 14

▲▼▲▼

CREATING A RESOURCE TEAM

The next several months went smoothly. Teams worked well together and associates pitched in to help each other out. Meanwhile, the work load was growing.

At one of the Team Rep Council meetings, Dan requested time to talk to the group.

"I know you've noticed the growing workload and the amount of overtime we've all had to put in. I think we'll continue to grow, so we're looking into adding another press to the plant. In addition, the Jugglers are about stretched to our limits. We're looking for ways to take some of the load off. Also, the folks at the corporate office have asked us to identify candidates to visit or move to other plants in the future and help implement team concepts. All of these developments indicate that it's time to start hiring again.

"But the main reason I'm here today is to tell you that we're creating a Resource Team. It will consist of three to five associates who'll help coordinate major projects, assist in problem-solving activities, help teams when needed, and relieve the Jugglers of some their responsibilities. I'd like the team reps to develop the selection criteria for the Resource Team. We will then let anyone who is interested apply."

"Will these people be supervisors with the authority to tell the rest of us what to do?" asked Clyde.

"They will have no more authority than anyone else," replied Dan. "You all have the authority to tell others what to do if you are right and can convince them to do it. The Resource Team will act in the same way. They may have additional responsibilities for a selected project or program. That will depend on what comes up and what we specifically ask them to do."

The team reps developed and posted the criteria, requesting that those interested sign up for an interview. The applicants were expected to make a presentation based on why they should be considered for the job. The application period would be open for one week.

Susan approached Billy during lunch the next day. "Billy, this Resource Team is your big chance."

"Me? You've got to be kidding," said Billy. "They wouldn't pick me."

"They might," replied Susan. She began ticking his good qualities off on her fingers.

"You know the press as well as anyone, better than most. Your social skills have really taken off since the changeover task team. You have made significant contributions to the plant. Your attitude is great and you're certainly willing to learn. What about the travel and possibly relocating to another plant? Would that be a problem?"

RESOURCE TEAM MEMBER SELECTION CRITERIA

1. **Good Technical Skills:** knows procedures, cross-trained on all press functions, good trouble-shooting skills, demonstrated problem-solving ability.

2. **Good Social Skills:** works well as team member, proven performance as a rep or task team member, communicates well with people.

3. **Leadership & Management Skills:** ability to organize, knows our organization, good trainer/teacher, respected by others.

4. **Positive Attitude:** maintains positive frame of mind, proven willingness to learn and grow, shows pattern of continuous improvement.

5. **Organizational Requirements:** willing to travel and deal with the external environment, willing to relocate if required.

"I don't know. I've never had to travel before and I haven't really thought about moving. I'll talk to my wife tonight and see what she thinks," Billy said.

"Well, you think about it, too. Remember, there's some extra money for this position. But the main reason to consider it is that you would be able to make a real contribution not only here, but maybe at some of Clear Lake's other plants as well."

"That's what makes me nervous," said Billy. "But I'll discuss it tonight at home with Judy. She's good at helping me see things clearly."

That evening Billy discussed the opportunity with Judy and she was enthusiastic. She convinced him to give it a shot. The next day Billy told Susan he was going for it.

Twelve other people applied. Billy spent the week working on what he would say. Finally, he met with the Jugglers to make his presentation.

"Hello everybody. I see Clear Lake as a human body," he said. He turned over his flip chart to a picture of a body with various parts labeled.

"The heart of our operation is the press, the lungs are the gluer, the brains are the teams—the people. But the lifeblood of this organization is communication and cooperation. To me, a Resource Team member would serve as a trainer who gets all the parts working together like an Olympic champion.

"When you put all of the teams together, we really are like a family." He turned over the flip chart and said, "The skills a Resource Team member needs are those that make a good family work.

> **F** = Facilitation Skills
> **A** = Ability & Aptitude
> **M** = Management Skills
> **I** = Involvement
> **L** = Learning Continually
> **Y** = Yearning to Be the Best

"With a body or a family, no single part is as strong as the whole thing working together. I want to help this plant's body and the Clear Lake family be the best they can be. Thank you very much."

"That was a great presentation, Billy," said Dan. "I think you've really captured what we are looking for in a Resource Team member. Any questions for Billy?" he asked the Jugglers.

Craig asked, "How would you help a team improve without acting like a supervisor?"

"I've wrestled with that issue on my own team and the task team I was on," said Billy. "By trial and error I found out the wrong way is to get mad and tell people they're wrong. That only makes them defensive and resistant to change.

"I've learned from Susan that the best way to communicate is to be a good listener. From my own experience, when I began to realize that people here really cared what I thought, I was ready to hear them out, too. So I guess when people are ready to listen, you give them facts and data, and demonstrate the improvements yourself."

When there were no other questions, Dan wrapped things up. "Thanks for your presentation, Billy. I can see that you put a lot of thought into it. We'll let you know what we decide next week."

▲▼▲▼

Billy was selected as one of the four members of the Resource Team. Alpha Team met to congratulate him.

"I'm so proud of you, Billy," said Susan.

"I owe a lot of it to you, coach," Billy said, hugging her. "And to you three," he added, gesturing to Karen, Clyde, and John. "Working with you guys has been one of the best experiences of my life."

"When do you start?" asked John.

"In about three months," said Billy. "I don't want to leave Alpha Team. I'll really miss you all."

Clyde said, "Dan said there will be a couple of announcements before the new team gets going."

"I wonder what that's all about?" mused Susan.

▲ Part V
▼ Transforming

Chapter 15

▲▼▲▼

PLANT EXPANSION
AND TEAM REFORMATION

Dan called a special meeting of the Jugglers.

"We've finally got approval from corporate to expand, so we'll be adding a third press. In addition, we'll be upgrading our existing presses from four colors to eight colors. As a result, we're going to have to hire twenty-five to thirty people."

"Does this mean we need to restructure all the teams?" asked Annette.

"I think so," said Dan. "With that many new people, we're going to have to spread our talent around."

"Maybe we should use this opportunity to consider establishing fixed shifts," Craig said. "A number of people have said rotating shifts are a big reason that more people aren't interested in working here."

"We could take a survey on shift preferences," said William, "and at the same time find out which people would like to work together. Then when we reform the teams, we can try to match up people according to their preferences."

CLEAR LAKE ORGANIZATION

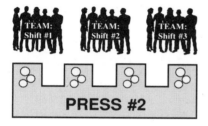

PRESS #1

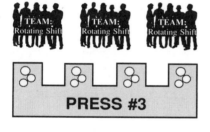

PRESS #2

PRESS #3

GLUER

(All teams report to the Jugglers.)

"Okay," said Dan. "It sounds like a good idea. Let's get to it."

At the next general plant meeting, Dan announced the upcoming changes and handed out the surveys. When all the surveys were in, Annette sorted through them and tabulated the results. At the next meeting of the Jugglers, she reported her findings.

"It looks like about two-thirds want fixed shifts and the remainder prefer rotating shifts. So I thought maybe we could have two presses with fixed-shift teams and one press with rotating-shift teams."

"That's an innovative solution," Dan said. "Let's try it and see what happens."

Dan presented the Jugglers' proposal to the plant.

"The responses from the surveys were mixed. Some of you want fixed shifts, and some would prefer to continue rotating, so we've come up with a solution that might satisfy just about everyone. We propose to have both—two presses manned by teams on fixed shifts and the third operated by rotating-shift teams.

"The new organization chart will look something like this." He turned on the overhead projector and showed the new structure.

"Any questions?" asked Dan.

"Will we remain on our existing teams?" asked Karen.

"It looks like we'll have to form all new teams," said Dan. "The surveys showed people on the same teams varying on which shift they preferred. In some cases we might be able to preserve two or three people on the same team. Annette tried to come up with some possible team combinations but it's hard to do without knowing the new associates."

"When will this happen?" asked John.

"We're going to start the hiring process now," said Dan. "So we'll shoot for three months from today."

Alpha Team met to discuss the new developments.

"It looks like we're breaking up," said Susan. "With Billy going to the Resource Team and the restructuring coming in three months, I guess we don't have much more time together."

"I really hate to see us split up," said Karen. "We've got one of the best teams in all of Clear Lake's plants."

"We can't look at it that way," said John. "Just think how much we improved when Susan and Billy joined the team."

"This will help us remember that we're all on the same big team," Clyde said.

"It's sure going to be different around here," Susan said sadly.

"Yeah," said Billy, nudging her. "We're back on the yellow brick road. Who knows what's waiting around the bend?"

EPILOGUE

Billy found Judy in the bathroom on her hands and knees. She was cleaning the toilet.

"Here, let me do that, Honey," he said, taking the rag from her. "You look tired."

Judy sat back on her heels in amazement. "What do you mean?"

Billy looked embarrassed. "Well, you always complain about the state I leave the bathroom in, but I never really thought about it till I had to do my share of housekeeping at the plant. Since each crew cleans up after itself on the press and we take turns cleaning the plant bathrooms, I see what a job it is and how much easier it is when we all do our part. Anyway, I've been thinking that the kids and I should do our part here, too, to free up some of your time."

Judy looked at Billy searchingly. "Billy, I can't believe the effect this job has had on you. For months I've wanted to say how nice it is to have you come home in a good mood. Your whole outlook on life just seems more cheerful. I've been so proud of you for all you have accomplished and how important you have become to the plant. But never in a million years did I think this would mean I was through cleaning toilets. I think this calls for your favorite supper."

Judy left the room. In the hallway she bumped into their ten-year-old daughter, Laura. "What's up?" Judy asked, noting the sullen expression on her daughter's face.

"Mom, everybody at my school has those new jeans and I want a pair, too," Laura whined.

"Now, Laura," Judy began. Billy surged to his feet to support his wife in this conflict, the praise Judy had given him for his attitude at home fresh on his mind.

"Laura, we've discussed this before. You know we can't afford to buy you every new thing that comes along. We set aside a certain amount of money for your school clothes for the whole year and we've got to stay within that budget," Billy said, trying to reason with her.

"But, Dad, why can't I choose my own clothes? Mom always makes me look like such a priss," she complained.

Billy was getting angry. Why couldn't these kids just accept that parents were the boss? That's the way his Dad handled things. Heck, that's the way the world works. Suddenly something Susan said came back to him.

He'd only been half-listening at lunch the other day, but she'd been talking about giving her son, Blake, a little more freedom. She'd said that though there were some rules that were not negotiable, like ones concerning safety, she was experimenting with giving the child more choices in the food he ate and the clothes he wore. "I'm working toward having a self-managing son," she'd joked .

Billy snapped out of it. Laura and Judy were looking at him strangely. "Listen, Laura, I'll have to talk to your mom about this, but how about this idea? You and your mom can sit down together and list the clothes you'll need for the whole year. We'll give you a budget and you'll have to get everything on the list. Maybe your mom can give us some pointers and you and I can go shopping."

Judy looked sharply at Billy. "Cross-training," he mouthed at her. "We can work it out, Laura, but from what I've seen of how you manage your allowance, you could use a little training in shopping. Anyway, after you've met the basic requirements for your wardrobe, any money left over will be yours to spend."

Billy looked at Judy to gauge her reaction. "It'll mean a little extra work on our part, Honey, but it will teach her something, too. When she finds out for herself how tricky it is to stay in those guidelines, then you won't be the bad guy anymore. Plus it wouldn't hurt to let her pick out things she likes. I can remember how much I wanted to look like everyone else back then."

Laura was practically jumping with excitement. She, too, looked at her mother.

Judy smoothed Laura's hair back from her forehead.

"I think your daddy's got a good idea there, Honey. We can start working on it today if you want to. Does this cross-training business mean I'm going to have to learn to fix the lawn mower?" she joked.

Billy laughed and left them talking about budget and quality. He went back to finish cleaning the bathroom, thinking about the concept of self-managing kids. When the phone rang, he went to answer it since Laura and Judy were in a "meeting."

"Billy, this is Carl, from the auto plant."

"Hey, Carl," Billy said. "Did you get reelected union president?"

"I sure did," Carl said. "In fact that's kinda what I'm calling about. Management at the plant's been talking about going to self-managing teams, and some of the guys are getting a little nervous. I wanted to see if you'd come to our next union meeting and fill us in."

"Well, sure, I guess. Is it still the first Tuesday of the month?"

"Yep," Carl confirmed, "Next Tuesday. Can we expect you?"

"I'll be there," Billy said.

Billy was reeling when he got off the phone. This had been a most unusual Saturday morning.

When he told Judy about Carl's request, she looked worried. "Do you think you should, Billy? Maybe you should check with Dan."

But Dan said it was fine. "Feel free to talk about how we work things out," he said. "When it comes to the actual work we do, though, just don't give away any trade secrets."

Tuesday evening, Billy was already opening the car door when he veered back into the house.

"Forget something?" Judy asked, looking up from her book.

"No, I remembered something," he said, grabbing a book and heading back for the car.

When he walked into the union hall, Carl ushered Billy to the front. "Billy has agreed to give us the scoop on self-managing teams. I think he'll be fair since he's been on both sides of the fence."

Billy cleared his throat nervously. "Last week I read an article that said that more than half of the one thousand biggest companies in the U.S. predict that they'll be switching to self-managing teams over the next ten years," he told the group. "And I have to tell you, I think it's a great idea."

"Well, let me just stop you right there and ask you to get specific, Billy," Carl said. "From what I hear, even though there aren't any supervisors, there is a lot of peer pressure.

And what about the added responsibilities—that's pressure too."

"And what about the policy on absenteeism," someone hollered from the back.

"Hold on," Billy said laughing. "Let me answer your questions one at a time.

"There is pressure to meet goals, I guess. But each team sets its own goals, based on what the whole team agrees. Nobody hands them down to us. And we want to do better because that means bigger gainsharing checks," he explained. "I didn't feel a lot of peer pressure, either. You gotta realize the plant spent two weeks giving us special training in how to work with others to solve problems. They didn't just drop it on us.

"The reason the whole thing works, though, is that everyone who works there really does have a say in the decisions that matter—the ones that affect us directly, as well as general plant policy. For example, you mentioned absenteeism. We employees wrote the policy on absenteeism at Clear Lake. We're all on salary, you know. There is no time clock to punch. If you're late and your team doesn't care, then nothing is said. My team did care because we were doing a great job meeting all our production goals and we wanted to maintain that standard.

"So we did write up one person who had an attendance problem. Now I guess you could call that peer pressure, but we talked to the person several times before acting. We tried to find out if there was a problem. With this person I mentioned, it turned out there was a personal problem.

"And that brings up another thing that's great about the concept of self-managing teams. The idea is that you work with whole people, not just robots. It's not the kind of job where you leave your brains at the door when you go in. That person with the problem got some help and is still with us.

"Getting to work wasn't a problem for me, though. I figured out that I missed less work there than I usually would in a year. My wife says she thinks it's because I'm happier all 'round. But it also helps that if there's something you just gotta do, you tell your team and arrange for someone to fill in. People there are willing to work with you and nobody hassles you about having a life outside the plant."

"So what else about this place made you so all-fired happy to be there?" asked someone.

Billy thought for a moment. "I don't have to raise my hand to go to the bathroom," he joked.

When the laughter died down he said, "Really. It matters to me that I'm trusted to do my job. When I need to go to the john, I go. I let someone on the team know, but nobody's timing me or worrying that I've taken an unauthorized break.

"Look, I brought this book, 'The Adventures of a Self-Managing Team.' A consultant at Clear Lake wrote this based on how the teams really function. This is my copy. I'll leave it with you and you can see for yourself how it feels to be on a self-managed team."

Appendices

CHARACTERISTICS OF SELF-MANAGING TEAMS

1. **SIZE:** Teams can be anywhere from 3 to 30 members. Most common are teams of 5 to 15 members.

2. **RESPONSIBILITIES:** Teams are usually responsible for the planning and production of a whole product or process, or a whole subassembly in the case of a complex product. They take the process from start to finish. They may have a wide range of technical, social, and administrative responsibilities. (See next section.)

3. **LEADERSHIP:** Leadership may vary from having no designated leader to one elected by the team to a formal leader/manager assigned by mangement.

4. **SKILLS:** Teams require members who are multiskilled in their technical abilities to carry out tasks. They need a relatively high level of interpersonal skills such as communicating, resolving conflicts, making group decisions, and problem solving. They also need administrative skills in managing meetings and performing whatever administrative responsibilities are assigned.

5. **TIME REQUIREMENTS:** Teams may meet daily, weekly, or as needed to coordinate work, solve problems, handle interpersonal issues, or perform administrative tasks. There is usually some blend of regular formal and informal meetings as required.

6. SUCCESS INGREDIENTS: Teams need clearly defined goals and expectations, clearly established roles and responsibilities, well-documented guidelines of behavior and ground rules, open communication in an atmosphere of trust and mutual respect, continuous learning and training in appropriate skills, patience and support by management, rewards tied to results, and a desire to continuously improve and innovate.

POTENTIAL AREAS OF RESPONSIBILITY

Responsibilities vary but may include:

1. **PRODUCTION:** Making or delivering the product or service.

2. **SCHEDULING:** Planning and coordinating production.

3. **QUALITY CONTROL:** Inspecting and ensuring high quality.

4. **MAINTENANCE:** Housekeeping and preventive maintenance.

5. **MATERIALS:** Obtaining raw materials, tools, parts, and supplies.

6. **SAFETY:** Ensuring safety practices and documenting problems.

7. **PROBLEM SOLVING:** Diagnosing and investigating problems.

8. **TRAINING:** Managing cross-training and all training activities.

9. **PERFORMANCE TRACKING:** Tracking production, quality, safety, costs, machine utilization, labor utilization, delivery, etc.

10. **BUDGETING:** Developing and monitoring costs.

11. **PERSONNEL ISSUES:** Tracking attendance, scheduling, time accounting, vacation schedules, etc.

12. **EMPLOYEE PERFORMANCE:** Managing selection, performance appraisals, discipline, layoffs, and termination.

13. **COMPENSATION:** Determining pay levels and coordinating raises, gainsharing, recognitions, and other rewards.

14. **OUTSIDE RELATIONSHIPS:** Dealing directly with vendors, customers, or other outside parties.

ORGANIZATION DESIGN ISSUES

When designing or redesigning an organization using self-managing teams, the following issues should be carefully considered before implementation:

1. **EXTERNAL FACTORS:** Markets, customer requirements, vendors, competitors, owners, organization history, and resources.

2. **STRATEGY:** Organization mission, management philosophy, key goals and objectives, operating strategies, and long-term and short-term plans.

3. **TECHNICAL SYSTEMS:** The way products and services are produced and the methods and systems needed to do it, including tasks, technologies, and facilities.

4. **STRUCTURAL SYSTEMS:** How people are organized, including both formal and informal systems.

5. **DECISION MAKING & INFORMATION SYSTEMS:** How decisions are made and how information flows throughout the organization.

6. **PEOPLE SYSTEMS:** How people are recruited, selected, trained, evaluated, disciplined, promoted, and developed.

7. **REWARD SYSTEMS:** How people and their contributions are recognized and rewarded, both formally and informally.

8. **RENEWAL SYSTEMS:** How the organization evaluates and improves itself.

9. **RESULTS:** How the organization performs in terms of customer satisfaction, technical performance, people performance, and business results.

IMPLEMENTATION STEPS

Most organizational design or redesign efforts use an implementation methodology similar to the following steps:

1. **FORM A STEERING COMMITEE:** A Steering Committee is generally made up of key people from top management, unions, or other critical areas of the organization. Their role is to establish the overall guidelines, to manage the process, and to approve recommendations.

2. **ESTABLISH A DESIGN TEAM:** A Design Team consists of key representatives from all areas of the organization to be designed. Their role is to analyze the existing state of the organization and to develop recommended changes. Their activities would include steps 3–6.

3. **ENVISION THE FUTURE:** Study and learn about what other organizations are doing. Develop a project game plan. Create a vision in broad terms of what the future state of the organization might be like.

4. **ANALYZE THE PRESENT STATE:** Analyze the existing state of the organizational systems and the issues outlined in the previous section.

5. **DEVELOP DESIGN RECOMMENDATIONS:** Prepare suggestions and design recommendations for all of the systems in question.

6. **DEVELOP TRANSITION PLANS:** Prepare implementation plans to guide the organization from the present to the future state. Report recommendations to the Steering Committe for approval.

7. **IMPLEMENT RECOMMENDATIONS:** Implement the transition plans, provide whatever training and education is required, and monitor the results. Implementation may begin with a pilot area with a subsequent roll-out to the rest of the organization.

8. **EVALUATE RESULTS:** Study the benefits and problems as a result of implementation. Get feedback from the organization. Develop a plan of continuous improvement and renewal.

IMPLEMENTATION SUGGESTIONS

1. **ALLOW ENOUGH TIME:** These efforts generally take from 6 months to 2 years before implementation depending on the size and complexity of the organization. Do your homework well!

2. **CREATE YOUR OWN SOLUTION:** No two organizations are alike and every organization requires its own customized design.

3. **GET SOME GOOD HELP:** Hire someone, either permanently or on a consulting basis, who has been through this process before and knows the issues and pitfalls to watch for.

4. **BE FLEXIBLE & INNOVATIVE:** Don't be afraid to examine and challenge any existing rule, procedure, structure, program, or philosophy. The most successful organizations have generally been the ones with the most innovative approaches.

5. **COMMUNICATE:** Make sure everyone understands what is happening and how it will affect them. Solicit as much input as possible from everyone involved and establish an open dialogue throughout the process.

6. **ANTICIPATE AN ADJUSTMENT PERIOD:** The changes will usually affect everyone, and for some people the effect will be dramatic. Resistance to change is a natural human trait, so expect it and be prepared to deal with it.

7. **BE PATIENT:** It will generally take several years to see the process through to fruition. Impatience, frustration, and taking short-cuts are the main enemies of success.

8. **DO IT:** Take the plunge! Be bold and innovative. The rewards are well worth the work.

STAGES OF TEAM DEVELOPMENT

Teams go through a series of predictable stages as they develop into maturity. Understanding these phases and helping teams move through them is essential to making teams fully functional.

STAGE 1 — START-UP ("FORMING"): When teams first come together, they must go through an orientation period. During this time, members are anxious about what their team will be like. They may be confused about what is happening and look for common areas of interest with each other. All members are individually preoccupied by the question of how they fit into the team and whether they will be accepted by the others. The whole team addresses the issues of goals, expectations, and tasks to be done.

STAGE 2 — CONFLICT ("STORMING"): As teams begin to develop common expectations, they go through a period of frustration and disagreement among the members. There is usually significant conflict around the issues of leadership, power, control, and influence. All members are wrestling with the question of how much relative influence they will exert on the team, as well as who they will allow to influence them. There may well be a "power struggle" between dominant members. The team must resolve the issue of how leadership and power will be distributed. Roles and "spheres of influence" need to be clarified.

STAGE 3 — TEAMWORK ("NORMING"): As roles are clarified, teams move through a period when a variety of conflicts and issues are resolved and norms of behavior are established. Functional relationships among members are developed, and disagreements are negotiated. Each member begins to understand his or her own strengths and weaknesses on the team, allowing them all to lead and follow where it is appropriate. Stronger bonds begin to develop among the members, and they become more interdependent as a group.

STAGE 4 — ACHIEVEMENT ("PERFORMING"): As teams mature into cohesive units, they enter the stage where they can focus on performance and results. Members are realistic in their expectations, major conflicts have been resolved, norms of behavior have been clarified, and attention is directed toward achievement. Productivity and continued team development are now the primary issues. Members work together in constructive ways to achieve common goals. Conflicts that arise are addressed and resolved according to common ground rules and guidelines.

STAGE 5 — CHANGE ("TRANSFORMING"): Depending on the circumstances, teams may have to deal with periods of significant change. Types of changes that may occur include losing or adding members, redefining a team's primary mission, or a total break-up of the team. Any of these changes will have a major impact on the team and will force members to address their fundamental expectations, goals, norms, and ground rules. In many cases, teams will "regress" to one of the previous stages and work their way back to "Achievement."

COMMENTS: All teams will generally go through all stages. Team development is similar to the the growth of an individual who goes through childhood, adolescence, young adulthood, and mature adulthood. The speed at which teams move through these stages may vary, depending on their size, the complexity of the jobs, the personalities of the members, and the circumstances of the situation. They can develop faster if they are given the appropriate training, time to deal with issues, and support as they move through the stages.

NOTE: Several models of group development are available in the literature. This model is the result of over fifty studies by Tuckman (1965).

REFERENCES AND
ADDITIONAL READING

Blanchard, K., Carew, D., & Parisi-Carew, E. (1990). *The one minute manager builds high-performing teams.* New York: William Morrow.
This book explores the stages of team development and how to vary leadership style at each stage for best performance.

Bucholz, S., & Roth, T. (1987). *Creating the high-performance team.* New York: John Wiley.
This book addresses the key characteristics of high-performing teams and how to develop each characteristic.

Orsburn, J.D., Moran, L., Musselwhite, E., & Zenger, J. (1990). *Self-directed work teams: The new American challenge.* Available from San Diego: Pfeiffer & Company.
This book outlines issues and methods for making self-directed work teams successful.

Pasmore, W.A. (1988). *Designing effective organizations: The sociotechnical systems perspective.* New York: John Wiley.
This book outlines the theory and practice of the sociotechnical approach to work redesign.

Tuckman, B.W. (1965). Developmental sequence in small groups. *Psychological Bulletin, 63,* 384-399.